The Secret
of the
Village Fool

Written by Rebecca Upjohn
Illustrated by Renné Benoit

Second Story Press

Milek and his brother, Munio, lived in a sleepy little village in Poland. One spring day their mother gave them a pot of soup, a loaf of bread, and some old clothes.

"Take these to Anton Suchinski's house," she said.

"I don't want to go there, Mama. Anton is *strange*. He talks to animals," said Milek.

"He talks to animals *and plants*," said Munio, who was three years older and knew more about everything.

But Mama's expression said they were going, whether they wanted to or not. She put her hands on her hips. "Anton may have his own way of doing things but he is a good man. And right now he's hungry." She shooed them out the door. "Tell him the soup is made from vegetables only. Come straight home. I don't want you wandering around the village."

When the brothers reached Anton's tiny house, they found him outside tending his garden. He smiled when he saw them. "Oh, my dears, how nice to see you." He was only slightly taller than Munio. His patched-up clothes smelled of earth, and his eyes were as bright as a bird's.

"Mama sent you soup and bread," Munio said. "And these." He held up two of their father's old shirts and a jacket.

Milek hovered behind Munio, saying nothing. He had heard so many odd stories about this man. Anton couldn't read or write. People said he thanked the sun and rain for growing his plants. They said he never ate meat. And they said he put out bowls of sugar water to feed the flies—as if there weren't enough flies already. People called him the village fool.

"Mama said to tell you the soup is all vegetables," said Munio.

"She is kind to remember," said Anton. "And the bread smells wonderful. Please tell her I thank her."

"How come you don't eat meat?" Milek blurted. Munio glared at him. But Milek wanted to know if the stories about Anton were true.

Anton's eyes crinkled as his smile widened. "Would you want to be someone's supper?"

"No!"

"Neither do the animals. Life is precious. No one should take it away."

Milek didn't know what to say to that.

"It's a long walk home. Would you like to share in this fine feast?"

Milek liked the idea but Munio shook his head. "We can't stay. Mama would be worried."

As the boys said good-bye, a neighbor who was walking past the yard stopped and stared at them. Munio pulled Milek back. They knew the man. Tata, their father, had warned them to keep out of his way.

"Watch out who you choose as your friends, Suchinski," the man said. "Those boys are Jews. I'd stay away from them if I were you."

Anton's smile disappeared. "That's an ugly thing to say."

"You really are a fool, aren't you? You are in for a surprise, you and your weird ideas. War is coming. When Hitler's armies arrive here, these Jews will be in trouble. Their friends will be in trouble too. You'll see!" He laughed and walked away.

Milek felt a knot in his stomach. "What does he mean? What war? Who is Hitler?"

Munio grabbed Milek's arm. "We have to go home. *Now!*"

"I will walk with you," said Anton, looking troubled.

After his fine supper of bread and soup, Anton watched the sun set and thought about his young friends. Adolf Hitler, the ruler of Germany, wanted to conquer all of Europe. Hitler and his Nazi soldiers hated Jewish people. Would they really come to this village? If they did, what would happen to Milek and Munio and their family, and to all the other Jewish people? Could anyone help them?

He sat in his thinking chair long after dark, worrying, worrying.

That summer the war did reach their village. Explosions thundered in the distance and war planes crisscrossed the sky. Bombs fell everywhere. Then the Nazis arrived. Columns of soldiers marched in, with tanks and big guns, and took charge. Not long after, they began to arrest Jews.

Early one morning, Milek woke to the sound of someone sobbing in the next room. He and Munio crept out to find Mama sitting with her arm around Eva, a family friend. Tears poured down the young woman's face as she spoke.

"They are gone! My whole family! My mother sent me outside to hide from the soldiers. When I came back, our house was empty. Everyone was gone."

"Things are very bad," said Tata. "The Nazis have ordered all the Jews in the village to go to the synagogue. There is a rumor that the soldiers are going to take away all the boys."

Mama gasped. Munio stared at Tata in disbelief. "They can't just take us away. They can't! I won't go—"

"Mama," cried Milek, running to her. "I want to stay with you!"

Tap-tap-tap. They all heard it. Someone was knocking at the back. "Pretend we're not here," whispered Mama, but Tata was already opening the door.

There stood Anton, holding a small bundle of clothes. "Oh, my dears, I'm glad you are still here," he said as he stepped inside. "I am so afraid for you. I have a plan to keep you safe. But you have to leave tonight." He caught sight of Eva. "You must come too," he said.

They all stared at him—funny Anton—poor Anton—Anton who fed flies—offering to save them. What could he possibly do?

Tata shook his head. "It is kind of you to offer, Anton, but we cannot accept. If the Nazis find out you are helping us. . .they will kill you."

Anton smiled. "Why would they bother with me? I am just the village fool—everyone thinks so. But I have a plan. You must trust me."

Tata hesitated and then nodded. "All right, Anton. Thank you."

"Come to me tonight," said Anton. He handed the clothing to Mama. "For the boys—a disguise." He slipped out the door as Mama shook out the clothes: two dresses and two kerchiefs.

Milek squawked. "I'm not wearing *those*! They're girls' clothes."

"Those clothes may save your life," said Eva quietly.

Munio suddenly understood what she meant, and he reached for a dress. "Come on, Milek," he said, as Mama helped him put it on. Scowling, Milek let Eva help him into the other one.

They heard shouting outside. Munio ran to the window and peeked out. "The soldiers are making all the Jewish families leave their homes," he said.

Mama's hands shook as she tied a kerchief over Milek's hair. Munio tried to tie his own, but Eva had to show him how.

"Come," said Tata to Mama. "We'll take our *girls* to the synagogue." He rested his hand on Eva's shoulder. "All three of them."

When they reached the synagogue, they found the other Jewish families huddled together outside. The soldiers carried out the sacred scrolls of the Torah and burned them. Then they set fire to the synagogue.

Mama held tightly to Milek and Munio. Milek wanted to yell, *Why do you hate us so much?* One man was beaten when he tried to lead his family away. The soldiers fired their guns into the air and threatened to shoot anyone who refused to stay and watch the synagogue burn.

Then the Nazis dragged all the boys from their families and forced them into a line. Milek and Munio stood with Eva and the other girls. Would the dresses really fool the soldiers? Milek's heart thumped so loudly he was terrified he'd be discovered. He closed his eyes and felt his brother take his hand. Munio was trembling too.

The soldiers marched the line of boys away, ignoring the pleading and wailing of their families. How could this happen, here in their own village?

"As soon as it gets dark," whispered Tata, "we will go to Anton."

That night they crept through the streets, passing broken buildings and stumbling over rubble. Every shadow looked like a soldier, and every barking dog made them jump. Sounds of weeping came from many houses. The smell of fire hung in the air. Milek slid his hand into Eva's. Tears had dried on her face, but she held her head high. He wanted to be brave too, but as he looked back, he clung tighter to her hand.

They slipped into the forest. Tata led them through the trees toward the edge of the village. As church bells rang through the dark, Mama stopped suddenly to hug Milek. "Midnight. It's your birthday." she whispered. He had just turned eight years old.

Anton opened the door and drew them quickly inside. He led them up to his attic. A girl, a few years older than Munio, was already there. She shrank back into the corner.

"This is Zipora," said Anton. "Her family was taken away last night."

Mama spoke softly to Zipora, and Eva stroked her hair. Milek stared at the girl, with her big, frightened eyes, and struggled to swallow the lump in his throat. Eva's family had been torn apart, and now Zipora's. Would his family be next?

As if sensing his thoughts, Anton said, "We are going to prepare a hiding place for you. A place where no one will ever, ever find you. We are going to dig down into the earth and make you a new home under the ground."

Night after night, while the others hid in the attic, Tata and Anton snuck out into the garden. In the root cellar, where Anton stored his onions and potatoes, they dug a short tunnel from one corner, down and back toward the house. At the end of the tunnel they dug another room, just big enough to hold six people.

"I want to help," said Milek.

"Me too!" said Munio.

"It's too dangerous," Mama said. "You will both stay in the attic with us."

Tata and Anton worked silently, always listening for soldiers on patrol, or the footsteps of other villagers eager to spy for the Nazis.

Anton and Tata dug with spoons and cups. As the earth

piled up, they carried it away in their pockets and spread it in the woods, where no one would notice.

At the back of the underground room they dug a narrow shaft up under the house, right through Anton's bedroom floor. Anton made a pulley from a rope and hook and hung it in the shaft. Then he covered the hole in his floor so no one who came inside would discover it.

"Why does everyone call Anton a fool?" asked Munio. "He's not a fool, he's smart. And he's brave."

Milek was silent, remembering how he had once felt about Anton.

At last the hiding place was ready. Anton gave them blankets and a kerosene lamp. "We will *all* survive this war," he promised.

Munio and Milek raced to be the first inside their new home. But their excitement quickly faded. The hideout was just a damp hole. Its walls were made of dirt held up by a few boards. The air was musty.

"It smells like worms!" said Milek, wrinkling his nose. "I don't like it!"

"We have to live in here?" asked Munio.

Zipora said nothing, but she looked miserable too. Once Eva, Mama, and Tata crawled in after them, there was no room to move. Only Milek was short enough to stand upright.

"I'm going out," said Milek.

"No," Tata said. "We have to stay inside."

"But there is no room. I can't *breathe*."

Tata took him in his arms. "I know this is hard for you. It's hard for all of us. But we can't go outside. People would see us and tell the Nazis. They would take you boys away—and maybe Mama and me, and Eva and Zipora too. And they would punish Anton for helping us. We must all be brave and stay out of sight."

"Why would anyone tell the Nazis?" demanded Milek. "We know everybody here. Why would anybody do that? Why do they hate us now?"

"Milek, some people. . ." Tata began, and then stopped. "I don't know," he said. "I just don't know."

Anton hid the tunnel exit in the root cellar under loose hay, so they could still get air. At night he lowered three buckets from his bedroom: one with food, one with water, and one to use as a toilet. They slept in two rows, with their feet touching.

One night they started itching and scratching. Their hiding place had been invaded by lice—bugs that live on blood—and they were soon covered in bites. Munio and Milek had a contest to see who could squish the most lice, but no matter how many they counted, there were always more.

After a few days, Munio asked, "Can we at least play up in the root cellar?"

"No," said Tata. "The Nazis are hunting everywhere for Jews. It's too risky. I'm sorry—you all have to stay here."

"But it's so *boring*," wailed Milek. "There's nothing to do!"

"We can play cat's cradle," said Zipora. She took the long ribbon from her hair, tied the ends together, and showed them how to form the shapes. They made up riddles that even Tata had trouble answering, and played rhyming word games with Mama. And every day, they named each missing member of Eva's and Zipora's families.

"Can we say Anton's name too?" asked Milek, one day. "He's like our family now, and he's all alone. What if he gets scared?"

"That is a fine idea," Mama said, hugging him.

At night, barely above a whisper, Tata told them stories of a world without war, where everyone lived safe and happy lives. People sang and danced in the sunshine, and feasted on honeycakes and dumplings. As Milek listened, he pressed hay into the dirt walls, making pictures to go with Tata's stories.

Outside, the war went on and on, with the drone of planes and the crack of gunfire. Summer turned to fall, then to winter, and then to spring. Underground, Anton's hideaways were stiff and sick from the dampness. Their joints grew swollen and sore. It became harder to dream of life above ground, and for the boys to remember the face of their protector. Now, Milek waited longingly for Anton's soft call, "My dears, how are you today?" which comforted them all.

Food grew scarce, and each day Anton walked farther to find it. He brought them raw beets, stale bread, and sometimes hot water with lumps of potato. Mama called it soup, but it wasn't.

Milek's belly ached. "I'm hungry, Mama," he cried.

"I know, little one," said Mama. "We all are. Anton is doing his best to find enough food for us. Sometimes he goes without his own supper, so we can have a little more."

"People are watching him," explained Tata. "If they see him carrying extra food, they will be suspicious. Anton is surrounded by danger all the time."

"He risks his life every day to keep us alive," said Mama.

"And he never gives up," said Eva touching Milek's cheek.

Milek cried silently and tried not to complain.

One evening, a loud voice came from outside. "Suchinski! I know you are hiding Jews."

Milek and Munio both recognized the voice. It was the neighbor who had threatened Anton all those months ago. Tata quickly blew out the lamp. He gave them rags to stuff in their mouths, to keep them quiet. No one dared move.

"The Nazis are paying good money for Jews—five hundred zlotys for an adult, and one thousand for a child," said the man. "Give up those people, and we'll share the money."

"I'm hiding no one," said Anton.

"Liar!" yelled the man. "I'll bet it's those brats who were in your yard that day. I'm warning you! I'll tell the soldiers, and their dogs will soon sniff out your precious friends. I'll keep that money for myself!"

That night, Anton spread dung mixed with herbs and pepper over the ground and down the steps into the root cellar.

At first light, the neighbor returned with some soldiers. "Where are the Jews?" shouted their captain. "We know you're hiding them! Tell us where, or you'll be sorry."

"There is no one here but me," said Anton.

"Tell us!" the captain demanded, pressing his gun against Anton's chest.

Anton thought of the six people underground, each one a precious life. He looked up into the soldier's eyes. "There's only me."

"He's lying!" said the neighbor.

"Look for them!" the captain ordered. The soldiers searched the house. They emptied closets and turned over furniture. They tore apart the attic. Then they went down into the root cellar.

Milek squeezed his eyes shut, sure that they were all about to be captured. The dogs sniffed and sniffed, but the dung mixture

Anton had spread fooled their noses. And the hay Anton had stacked over the tunnel entrance kept it hidden. The soldiers found nothing.

"We'll get the truth out of you," the captain said. "If you are lying, you will die!" The soldiers took Anton away.

Anton was gone for the rest of the day. And another day, and another. "Where is Anton, Mama?" Milek asked. "Is he safe?" But Mama had no answers and Milek cried, afraid for his friend.

After six days, a group of soldiers set up camp in Anton's yard. They rested in the root cellar. Light from their lantern filtered through the hay as they argued and joked. Milek smelled something—could it be chocolate?—and his mouth watered. How long had it been since he'd tasted anything like that? Metal snapped and clicked as the soldiers cleaned and reloaded their guns.

"Ah!" said a soldier. "I dropped a bullet." A small piece of metal fell into the tunnel and rolled all the way down, landing on Munio's foot. He froze, afraid to move. "Where did it go? It

must be here somewhere." The hay rustled as the soldier poked around.

Milek's heart pounded. Any moment now, they'd be discovered. They would all be taken away. He bit down on the rag in his mouth to keep from whimpering.

A shout came from outside and the soldiers hurried away. There was more shouting farther off, but Milek couldn't make out the words. Guns fired. Then silence fell. What was happening? Had Anton come back? Had the soldiers shot him?

Suddenly, there were footsteps. Someone was in the root cellar. The steps sounded louder and louder—and then the hay was pulled away. A bright light flooded into their hiding place. Milek buried his face in Mama's side. The Nazis had found them!

But from behind the light came a sweet, familiar voice. "My dears! Oh, my dears, come out! You can come out, you are safe now! All the Nazis are gone!"

Munio pulled the rag from his mouth. "Anton!" he yelled. He crawled up the tunnel, through the root cellar, and outside. Milek followed, with the others close behind. They were so weak, after being cramped underground for so long, that Anton needed to help each one climb out. They stood with him, blinking in the light of a clear summer day. They felt the sun warm their faces. They breathed in the clean air. Were they really free, after all those long months?

With tears streaming down their faces, Mama and Tata said to Anton, "How can we ever thank you?"

"We thought they shot you," Eva whispered. Anton wrapped his arms around them all.

Milek looked up at Anton's shining face. "You really did save us!"

Anton smiled. "My dear, how could I not save you? I knew in my heart it was what I was meant to do. Life is precious— every life." And he took Milek's hand, and held it gently in his own.

What Happened After

In July of 1944, the Nazis were driven from Zborów, Milek and Munio's village (then in Poland, now in Ukraine). The six survivors remained with Anton, slowly recovering from their year in hiding, until the war ended in 1945.

Milek and Munio Zeiger moved with their parents to the United States in December 1949. The boys changed their names: Milek to Shelley, and Munio to Michael. The two brothers still live in the United States today, with their wives, children, and grandchildren.

This is the entrance to the root cellar, which led to the hiding place below.

Before the war, Eva had been engaged to a man who had left Poland to find work in Uruguay, in South America. After the war, her fiancé traced her through the Red Cross and the Jewish community. Reunited with him in Uruguay, Eva married and had two sons, Emanuel and Baruch. The family later moved to Israel. Today, Emanuel and his wife divide their time between work in Canada and family in Israel. Baruch lives with his family in Israel, where he also works.

Eva Adler died in 2005.

Zipora Stock moved to Israel, where she married. She and her children and grandchildren still live there.

The Zeigers tried to persuade Anton to move with them to the United States, but he refused to go, telling them he "wanted to die where he was born." For years, Mrs. Zeiger sent him packages of canned food and clothing. Because Anton could not read or write, he dictated his letters to a neighbor. On each letter he drew a flower, so that the Zeigers would know the letter was from him.

During the 1960s, Anton's letters stopped arriving. The Zeigers did everything they could to find Anton, but it was difficult to get news from

Zborów. Workers from the Red Cross searched, but they could not locate him. His house was empty, and no one knew what had happened to him. The Zeigers sadly concluded that he must have died.

Mr. Zeiger (Tata) died in 1971.

In 1988, Shelley (Milek) Zeiger met a man from the Zborów region who agreed to look for Anton one last time. This time, the search was successful. The Zeigers discovered that Anton was living in extreme poverty. They had a new house built for him, and arranged to have people care for him for the rest of his life.

The next year, Shelley, Michael, and their mother traveled to Zborów, and came together, once again, with the man who had saved their lives. One thousand people from the town celebrated with the Zeigers and Anton. The "village fool" had become the village hero.

Finally, in 1988, after years of searching, a man Shelley knew found Anton. Everyone had believed he was dead.

Shelley (Milek), Mama, Anton, and Michael (Munio) in 1989
when the Zeigers traveled back to their village to see Anton again.

The villagers of Zborów celebrated with Mama and Anton at a
ceremony held to honor him. Anton had become the village hero.

After this reunion in Zborów in 1989, Anton and Mama (Mrs. Zeiger) met again when Anton visited the United States.

Now there is a memorial, erected by the Zeiger family, to the Jewish people killed in Zborów.

In 1992, reunited at a ceremony with Michael Zeiger, Eva Adler, Zipora Stock (now Schindelheim), and their families, Anton Suchinski was recognized as Righteous among Nations—a Righteous Gentile—at Yad Vashem, the Holocaust Memorial and Museum in Jerusalem. His name was added to the Wall of Honor in The Garden of the Righteous.

Eva, Anton, and Zipora with Michael behind them at the Yad Vashem ceremony in 1992.

Michael, Eva, Zipora, and their families surround Anton with the Wall of Honor in The Garden of the Righteous behind them.

Mrs. Zeiger (Mama) died in 1997.

Anton Suchinski died in 2001 at the age of ninety-six.

The medal he received at Yad Vashem is engraved with a Jewish saying: "Whosoever saves a single life, saves an entire universe."

Anton's name is included on the Wall of Honor in The Garden of the Righteous.

Further Reading:

Zeiger, Shelly, and Maryann McLoughlin. *The Wheel of Life: A Memoir.* Margote. Comteq. 2012.

www1.yadvashem.org/yv/en/righteous/stories/sukhinski.asp

Acknowledgements
I am grateful to the Ontario Arts Council for supporting the writing of this book through the Writers' Reserve Grant program.

I could not have written this story without the generous assistance of Margie Wolfe, Shelley Zeiger, Emanuel Adler, Michael Zeiger, Maryann McLoughlin, Gena Gorrell, Carolyn Jackson, Irena Steinfeldt, Wieslaw Michalak, Sarae Snyder, Harris, Emmett and Don Snyder, Connie Harvey, Jann Everard, Laurel Dee Gugler, Susan Chapman and Melissa Kaita.
—R.U.

For Margie and for Anton
—R.U.

For my family
—R.B.

LIBRARY AND ARCHIVES CANADA CATALOGUING IN PUBLICATION

Upjohn, Rebecca, 1962-
The secret of the village fool /
written by Rebecca Upjohn Snyder ;
illustrated by Renné Benoit.

ISBN 978-1-926920-75-7

1. World War, 1939–1945—Poland—Juvenile fiction.
2. Holocaust, Jewish (1939–1945)—Poland—Juvenile fiction.
I. Benoit, Renné II. Title.

PS8641.P386S43 2012   jC813'.6   C2012-902881-9

Text copyright © 2012 by Rebecca Upjohn Snyder
Illustrations copyright © 2012 by Renné Benoit

Editor: Gena Gorrell
Design: Melissa Kaita

Photos on pages 30/34/35/36 used with permission
© the Adler family collection and Yad Vashem
Photos on pages 31/32/33/34/36 courtesy the Zeiger family

Printed and bound in China

Second Story Press gratefully acknowledges the support of the Ontario Arts Council, the Ontario Media Development Corporation, and the Canada Council for the Arts for our publishing program. We acknowledge the financial support of the Government of Canada through the Canada Book Fund.

Published by
SECOND STORY PRESS
20 Maud Street, Suite 401
Toronto, ON
M5V 2M5
www.secondstorypress.ca